Waiting in Joyful Hope

Daily Reflections for Advent and Christmas
2004–2005

Robert F. Morneau

LITURGICAL PRESS

Collegeville, Minnesota

www.litpress.org

Cover design by Ann Blattner.

1   2   3   4   5   6   7   8

ISBN 0-8146-2894-X

Introduction

Every liturgical season has its lexicon, its vocabulary, that helps us to see the working of God in a particular time of the Church's year. In the Easter season we hear a great deal about resurrection, new life, and a thousand alleluias. In Ordinary Time we ponder the way of Jesus: the way of compassion, forgiveness, and love. Advent too has its lexicon, its special dictionary pointing us to the Christmas mystery and beyond. For me those Advent words are "come," "hope," and "nativity."

Come

As the Carmelite poet Jessica Powers accurately observes: "Come is the love song of our race." Our God is always an approaching, impinging God who longs to be with the people created out of divine love. This God comes to us through the great mysteries of our faith: creation, redemption, and sanctification. In this Advent season we request that we might experience more deeply this triune God who made us, heals us, and continues to guide us still. It is not that God is absent but rather that we must dispose our hearts, ready once again, to encounter a God who is already in our midst.

So we pray: "Come, Holy Spirit, come." "Come, Lord Jesus, come." "Come, Father of the poor." That is, come into our minds and hearts so that we might be people who understand the divine plan and who love so deeply as to give ourselves away. Through the sacraments we place ourselves at the intersection of grace and are privileged to encounter the living and true God.

Hope

Our God is a promise-maker; our God is a promise-keeper. The promise made is not one of a life free from trouble and suffering. Rather, the promise is one of presence: "I will be with you always." Advent is a season of hope in that we await the fulfillment of that promise. Advent is a season of expectation as we anticipate the Lord's arrival into our consciousness, our hearts, our history. Expectancy and longing are the first cousins of hope.

But we can wait in the wrong way, that is, with high anxiety and with false expectations. We can become discouraged and impatient in that we want to experience God in "our" way and in "our" good time. At such moments it is good to recall the simple preposition "with." "I am with you always." Hope supported by faith leads to charity.

Nativity

What we wait for and long for is new life. Jesus is that life, the manifestation of the mystery of God. In him we see the face of God; in him we experience the power of the Spirit. Born of Mary our Lord comes into history to share that divine life with us. This grace, this friendship with God, is the greatest blessing possible. Just as Mary conceived and nurtured the Word, we too, during this holy season, are to conceive and nurture and, yes, give birth to the Lord of Lords, and the Prince of Peace.

What excitement first-time parents experience as they await the nativity of their child. What excitement and possible anxiousness as they know their whole life will now be different. Advent well celebrated means change. When Jesus enters our soul and the community nothing remains the same. All is made new. Jesus, now living in us in an intentional way, transforms all of creation.

FIRST WEEK OF ADVENT

November 28: First Sunday of Advent

Advent Words

Mass: Isa 2:1-5; Rom 13:11-14; Matt 24:37-44

Scripture:
Jesus said to his disciples:
  "Stay awake, therefore! You cannot know the day your
    Lord is coming." (Matt 24:42)

Reflection: Advent words: stay awake . . . watchful . . .
be prepared . . . coming! This is the season of expectation,
God once again is breaking into history not only in our liturgical celebrations but also in the daily events of our life.
If we are attentive and discerning, we will catch the sun-
beams of grace and the patches of holiness.

Isaiah was one of those prophets who were wide-awake
and filled with expectation. His desire was to walk in the
light of the Lord, to climb God's mountain, to be a witness
to peace. His vision stirs us still as he speaks of swords
being beaten into plowshares and deadly spears transformed into pruning hooks. Even our technology will serve
the coming of God's kingdom.

St. Paul was a watchful, prepared apostle. His experience
of Advent transformed his life as he put on the Lord Jesus
and turned from deeds of darkness. He pleads with the Ro-
mans (and us) to wake from sleep and be attentive to God's

coming. One can feel the urgency in his message and his longing that everyone might come to know the Lord Jesus.

Meditation: What Advent word does the Lord want you to live out during this season? In what ways does God come into your life?

Prayer: Lord Jesus, you call us to be vigilant, watchful people. During this season of Advent help us to be attentive to your voice, responsive to our love. Like Isaiah may we walk in the light of your love; like St. Paul, may we put on the armor of light and faith. Send your Spirit into our hearts that we may be transformed; send your Spirit into our broken world that it may know your peace and justice.

November 29: Monday of the First Week of Advent

The Gift of Faith

Mass: Isa 2:1-5; Matt 8:5-11

Scripture:
Jesus showed amazement on hearing this and remarked to his followers,
   "I assure you, I have not found this much faith in Israel."
      (Matt 8:10)

Reflection: The centurion who approached Jesus with the request that his serving boy be healed is a noble character. This man of authority had compassion for a servant who suffered great pain; this centurion possessed humility in realizing his unworthiness in the presence of Jesus; this leader had the gift of faith for he truly believed that Jesus had the power and the desire to heal the sick.

   To cause amazement in the heart of Jesus is itself amazing. Often Jesus encountered doubters and skeptics, critics and disbelievers, hypocrites and frauds. But on this day our Lord met someone who had the deep conviction that Jesus had the power and will to alleviate the suffering of the servant boy. This deep conviction is what we call faith. It also is characterized by trust and submission. Though possessing political authority this centurion knew that God had the ultimate authority and power over life and death.

Advent is a season of faith. As a pilgrim people we approach the Lord with our request to live deeply our faith commitment. On this precarious and perilous journey we ask the Lord to heal our broken world and to empower us to recognize the Lord's presence in the suffering and lonely. Advent faith is a trustful reliance on God's help. Advent faith is an awareness that, though unworthy, we long to offer the Lord our gracious hospitality. Come, Lord Jesus, come!

Meditation: Does our faith cause amazement in the heart of Jesus?

Prayer: Jesus, healer and redeemer, we long for your coming into our lives. Help us to believe in your abiding presence in word and sacrament. Help us to respond to your coming to us in the poor and suffering. Through your Spirit make our faith vibrant and overflowing in love.

November 30: Tuesday of the First Week of Advent

Seeing and Hearing

Mass: Isa 11:1-10; Luke 10:21-24

Scripture:
Turning to his disciples he [Jesus] said to them privately:
   "Blest are the eyes that see what you see. I tell you, many
      prophets and
   kings wished to see what you see but did not see it, and
      to hear what you
   hear but did not hear it." (Luke 10:23-24)

Reflection: Flannery O'Connor (1925–1964) was one of our great Catholic writers. Her three novels and short stories portray the action of grace in strange ways, through the lives of people who are not particularly attractive. In fact, many of her characters are grotesque and repulsive. But she knew what she was about and claimed that when you write for a culture that is blind and deaf you have to draw large distorted pictures and shout at the top of your voice. Her mission was to wake us up and help us to see and hear.

Jesus, in dealing with his culture and even with his own disciples, had the same struggle. There is a blindness and deafness that prevent us from encountering the truth and experiencing divine love. So ultimately God's truth and love will be made manifest on a cross. If we cannot see what that is about or hear the cry of abandonment from that naked tree, we are in real trouble.

Advent is a time of seeing and hearing. Jesus comes to us in the Scriptures, through the sacraments, and in the communities of the faithful. Hopefully, through the strength of the Holy Spirit, we will recognize his coming. Jesus speaks to us in the Gospel, in the teaching of the Church, and through the witness of the communion of saints. Hopefully, empowered by the Spirit, we will hear and respond to his voice.

Meditation: What obstructs your seeing, your hearing? How does God reveal to you the good news of love and mercy?

Prayer: Lord Jesus, you give sight to the blind and hearing to those who are deaf. Come into our lives these Advent days and help us to see the glory of the Father and to hear the cry of the poor. Send your Spirit of justice and mercy and peace into your world. Then we shall truly be your people, agents of your love and light.

December 1: Wednesday of the First Week of Advent

Divine Compassion

Mass: Isa 25:6-10; Matt 15:29-37

Scripture:
Jesus called his disciples to him and said:
  "My heart is moved with pity for the crowd." (Matt 15:32)

Reflection: A nurse in one of Chaim Potok's novels, *Davida's Harp,* constantly uses the refrain that she has to go where the suffering is. This seems to be the case with Jesus. He goes where the suffering is: to those who are burdened with demons and illness and disabilities. He is on the look-out for the people who find life heavy and offers to them his consolation and gift of life and love.

This mission of compassion is grounded in a deep solidarity. Jesus feels the pain of others. He refuses the self-protection of wealth and power, of prestige and status. Jesus emptied himself and took on our human nature in such a profound way that he knows from the inside what human suffering and pain is all about. He experienced hunger; he knew the exhaustion of work and travel; he had to deal with rejection and misunderstanding. His compassion flowed out of human experience and oneness with the rest of us.

During these Advent days we are invited to feed the hungry, to visit the imprisoned, to comfort those who mourn. When we are "moved with pity" we come to know the coming of Jesus into our lives. We meet Christ in a special way in the poor and abandoned, in the neighbor who just lost a spouse, in the person suffering from a broken relationship. Advent is a time to go where the suffering is and there we will meet the Lord.

Meditation: What is your response to the suffering of the world? Who are the people who have shown to you the Lord's compassion?

Prayer: Gracious and loving God, do not let our hearts be hardened. May we see in those who are hungry and thirsty, in those who are strangers and aliens, in those who are oppressed and lonely, the face of Jesus, your Son. Through your Spirit of pity and mercy, may we respond to our hurting sisters and brothers with tender sympathy. Grant this in Jesus' name.

Solid Mission

Mass: Isa 26:1-6; Matt 7:21, 24-27

Scripture:
Jesus said to his disciples:
"Anyone who hears my words and puts them into practice
is like the wise man who built his house on rock."
(Matt 7:26)

Reflection: Two things can be of great assistance in living the life of discipleship. The first is being clear about mission, what we are about as followers of Jesus. The second is to have a rule of life that keeps us on the Gospel path.

Our mission is to do God's will; it is a life of obedience to whatever the Lord asks of us. Jesus came that we might have life, life in great abundance (John 10:10). Our mission and God's will are connected to this giving life, to the sharing of God's love, to being a light to the nations. To build our lives on the rock of life, love, and light (three words for grace) is to demonstrate that one is a wise person.

As for a rule of life, we should have at the head of the list the principle of putting into practice whatever God's word calls us to do, be it forgiving an enemy, having compassion on the suffering, reaching out to the needy. Father Tim, a character in Jan Karon's Mitford series, is constantly saying: "Consider it done!" We too might have this as a rule of life in responding to God's requests: "Consider it done!"

Meditation: What is your mission in life? Do you have a rule of life?

Prayer: God of wisdom, share with us your vision of the kingdom. May we see clearly what our mission in life is and empower us through your Spirit to put into practice every word that comes from your heart. Often we build our lives on sandy ground; often we simply drift through time without a sense of purpose. Come to our aid so that this Advent may be a time of renewal and deeper commitment to your love and grace.

Confidence

Mass: Isa 29:17-24; Matt 9:27-31

Scripture:
Jesus said to them [two blind men],
   "Are you confident I can do this?"
   "Yes, Lord," they told him. (Matt 9:28)

Reflection: Blind trust is an amazing thing. We allow a surgeon whom we have never met to cut us open; we board a jet airliner and trust that the pilots will get us safely to our destination; we ask directions from a stranger with a sense that the information given will be accurate. Sometimes our trust and confidence is misplaced: the surgeon may not be competent; the plane may crash; the directions lead us down dead-end roads.

   The two blind men in the Gospel had some knowledge of Jesus and his healing ministry. They cry out to this Son of David for pity and healing. They came to him in faith and confidence, and as Jesus touched their eyes they were given a new vision. But they "saw" even before the cure, for they had the vision of faith that Jesus could grant them new life.

   During this Advent season we are to renew our confidence in the Lord's power to heal our blindness, our insensitivity to the needs of others, our narcissism. Our challenge is to be "caught up with him" as the blind men were and to cry out, day after day, "Have pity on us!" Confident that the Lord will heal us we can then venture forth to do our work of evangelization—telling others of the marvelous things that God has done for us.

Meditation: How deep is your trust? In what ways has Jesus touched your eyes?

Prayer: Jesus, Son of David, hear our cry for mercy. We have confidence in your power to heal us and set us free from the bondage of sin. Touch our eyes, bless our souls. May our faith be deep and abiding. Send us forth to spread the word of your saving love throughout the world.

Stewardship

Mass: Isa 30:19-21, 23-26; Matt 9:35–10:1, 6-8

Scripture:
He [Jesus] gave them these instructions: . . .
   "The gift you have received, give as a gift." (Matt 9:8)

Reflection: Stewardship is a whole way of life based upon conversion of heart. Stewardship is an expression of our discipleship. As one person said: "Stewardship is what I do after I say I believe." Stewards live a life of prayer, a life of service, and a life of sharing.

Stewardship is about gifts, gratitude, and generosity. This Gospel way of life flows from our image of God who is Giver, Given, and Giving (see Michael Downey's *Altogether Gift*). In a nutshell stewardship is to receive God's gifts with deep gratitude, to nurture and cherish those gifts responsibly, and then to share what God has given to us in justice and, far beyond that, in sacrifice. Jesus instructs his disciples that what they have received is to be shared with others.

In Psalm 116:12 we are given the stewardship question: "How shall I make a return to the Lord / for all the good he has done for me?" Stewardship is payback time; stewardship is translating our belief into practice. During this season of Advent we are invited to become aware of the greatest gift of all—our life in Christ. But this gift is not given just for us. It is to be shared with others thus turning our life of stewardship into a life of evangelization. Jesus is clear: "The reign of God is at hand!" Indeed, God's kingdom in Jesus is within us—the greatest gift of all. No better Christmas gift can be given than the sharing of our faith.

Meditation: What are the gifts that God has given to you? How do you share these gifts?

Prayer: God of so much giving, help us to emulate you. You have blessed us in so many ways and we offer you fitting praise by sharing "your" gifts with those around us. May we never take your gifts for granted; may we live with grateful hearts. One day may we return to you tenfold all that you have given to us. Through a life of generosity may we give you great glory.

SECOND WEEK OF ADVENT

December 5: Second Sunday of Advent

God's Way

Mass: Isa 11:1-10; Rom 15:4-9; Matt 3:1-12

Scripture:
"A herald's voice in the desert:
'Prepare the way of the Lord,
make straight his paths.'" (Matt 3:3)

Reflection: "I did it my way!" This lyric, made popular by Frank Sinatra, still echoes through our culture. It is so easy to get stuck on the road of consumerism, individualism, me-ism. What a far cry from the prophet's proclamation of making ready the "way" of the Lord.

What is God's way? It is the path trod by Jesus. His mission and ministry is ours, and we are to follow him whatever the cost. Jesus' way is the way of love, compassion, and forgiveness. Love means responding to God's will and the needs of our sisters and brothers. Compassion is the path of identifying with the joys and sorrows of others, making them our own. Forgiveness is passing on the mercy that God has bestowed on us in dealing with our sinfulness. This is the way of the Lord; this is the Gospel path.

There are obstacles, however. The path is often crooked because of the capital sins: pride, avarice, anger, envy, wrath, lust, gluttony, and sloth. Thus we hear John the Baptizer demand that we reform our lives because God's reign is approaching. We need the strength and power of the Holy Spirit if we are to respond adequately to the voice crying out in the desert: "Prepare the way of the Lord, make straight his path."

Meditation: What areas of your life are in need of "reformation"? If you and John the Baptist went out for lunch, what would be on your agenda for discussion?

Prayer: God of our salvation, it is through the grace of baptism and the forgiveness of sin that we experience your tender mercy. Help us to hear your word; empower us to follow your way. Do not let despair or pride prevent us from living in union with you. Open our ears to the prophets' words, and strengthen us in our commitment to follow your Son, Jesus. Grant this through your Spirit. Amen.

Healing

Mass: Isa 35:1-10; Luke 5:17-26

Scripture:
"I say to you, get up! Take your mat
with you, and return to your house." (Luke 5:24)

Reflection: The paralytic in today's Gospel is anonymous. So too are his friends who brought him to Jesus. But each of us can insert our name into the story, for each of us is in need of healing—physically, psychologically, morally, spiritually. No matter our age or nationality, our gender or employment, our education or occupation, we all stand in need of God's healing touch.

Our sins may be major (pride, brutality, disobedience) or minor (thoughtlessness, not caring enough, sulking). Wherever we are and whatever we are doing, Jesus wants to enter our life to instruct us in his way and to forgive our offenses. Jesus is teacher and healer; Jesus is friend and Messiah. If we do not come to him ourselves, hopefully friends will be there to lead us to our Lord. God's will is that we be whole and holy.

Once healed we are to "get up and walk." This walking is the road of evangelization, the true mission of the Church. What has been given us we are to share with others—the good news of our salvation in Jesus. It's not enough to return home to the kitchen table. We return to our neighbors and, filled with awe and astonishment, report to them what God has done in our lives—incredible things. By so doing we bring Jesus into the lives of other paralytics, sharing with them divine truth and healing. Such is the power of forgiveness; such is the power of God's mercy.

Meditation: In what ways has God healed you? How do we "heal" one another?

Prayer: Jesus, our teacher and healer, come once again to bring us your truth and wholeness. We stand in need of your mercy and wisdom. We seek the experience of your tender love. We praise you for the mystery of redemption, our salvation from sin and death. Help us to continue to see your astonishing works and send us forth to proclaim your abiding love. Grant this through the power and gift of the Holy Spirit. Amen.

December 7: Tuesday of the Second Week of Advent

Lostness

Mass: Isa 40:1-11; Matt 18:12-14

Scripture:
  Jesus said to his disciples:
  "A man owns a hundred sheep
  and one of them wanders away . . . ." (Matt 18:12)

Reflection: A phrase from the ever-popular "Amazing Grace," "I once was lost, but now am found. . . ." The composer of this hymn was John Newton, a slave trader, who was lost in the sin of exploitation and oppression. But the intrusions of grace transformed his life. He who was lost in sinful ways was found.

Grace is indeed amazing. If we are honest, all of us can identify with the lost sheep since all of us are sinners and stand in need of redemption. Jesus is the Good Shepherd who seeks us out by sending into our lives the Scriptures, the sacraments, and a faith community committed to a life in Christ. God is faithful and never gives up on us regardless of our wanderings down dead-end roads.

Several years ago an article was written decrying the fact that an attempt was being made to drop the word "wretch" from the lyrics of "Amazing Grace" ("Amazing grace, how sweet the sound, that saved a wretch like me. . . ."). What a mistake that would be since being separated from God is truly a wretched state of being. If the truth helps to set us free, then admitting to our true condition is a step on the road to salvation. Lost sheep are on the margin of death. Being found brings us back into life, the land of grace. Amazing is God's love for us.

Meditation: Have you ever been lost? Physically? Psychologically? Spirituality? Who came to find you? How did you get back "home"?

Prayer: Gracious and loving Shepherd, we need your guiding hand. So often we wander far from you, lost in foolish ways. We thank you for bringing us back home through reconciliation; we thank you for sending into our lives good shepherds who sought us out; we thank you for not giving up on us. May we in turn reach out to others who stray and, in joy, bring them back to you. In gratitude we make this prayer. Amen.

December 8: Solemnity of the Immaculate Conception

Abiding Presence

Mass: Gen 3:9-15, 20; Eph 1:3-6, 11-12; Luke 1:26-38

Scripture:
Upon arriving the angel said to her:
"Rejoice, O highly favored daughter!
The Lord is with you. Blessed are you among women."
(Luke 1:28)

Reflection: God was with Mary throughout her life. God was there when Mary was conceived and received the great gift of life. God was with Mary in the moment of her unique vocation of being asked to be the mother of Jesus. God was with Mary at the foot of the cross as she endured the agony of her Son's cruel death. This being "with," this grace of presence, is offered to all of us.

Not all of us, however, have the openness of Mary. Despite the fact of being afraid and not knowing what was happening, Mary's faith enabled her to say yes to what the Lord asked of her. Hers was a life of obedience, a deep listening and responding to God's will. Mary was the handmaid of the Lord and this sense of identity brought forth a profound commitment to God's request.

When Abraham was asked by God if he was willing to participate in the history of salvation Abraham did not say "What?" or "I will think it over." Rather, his response amounted to "Ready!" Mary was ready and willing and able to follow God's will. "Ready" was her graced response and was made possible because the Spirit of the Lord was *with* this servant of God. We are all the beneficiaries of her loving obedience.

Meditation: How do you react to the fact that Mary was afraid and ignorant? In what sense is Mary the mother of the Church? How can we imitate Mary in our times?

Prayer: Providential God, your hand is always at work throughout creation. From the very first moment of conception to the day we breathe our last you are with us. In preparing Mary to be the mother of Jesus, your Son, she was kept free from all sin. Help us to be open to your grace so that we too, like Mary, might be ready to say "yes" to the workings of your love and life. Keep us from sin on this perilous journey. May we one day celebrate with Mary and all the saints the mystery of your triune love. We ask this in the name of Jesus. Amen.

December 9: Thursday of the Second Week of Advent

Heeding and Hearing

Mass: Isa 41:13-20; Matt 11:11-15

Scripture:
Jesus said to the crowds:
"Heed carefully what you hear!" (Matt 11:15)

Reflection: God speaks to us in so many ways: the Scriptures, the teachings of the Church, daily experience, the intuitions of the heart. And the message is constant and demanding: love one another as I love you; fear not, I am with you; be compassionate and merciful. Unfortunately we "just don't get it" and remain in darkness and depression. We don't get it because we don't live it. Listening is only half our mission. The other half is implementation: do God's word in truth and love.

John the Baptist heard and heeded God's word. Already filled with joy in the womb of his mother Elizabeth, John lived a spirit-filled life as a prophet of the Lord. It cost him his life but such is the way of any disciple. Discipleship is following the Lord all the way to Calvary and beyond into the life of resurrection. But that following is essentially a life of radical obedience. John translated into action the plan God had for him: the proclamation of the truth and the preparing of the way of the Lord.

As Advent people we are recipients of John's prophetic ministry. During these dark days of December, we are constantly reminded of John's work as one of preparation. He made ready the way of the Lord. Listen to the word of his father Zechariah: "And you, O child, shall be called / prophet of the most High; / For you shall go before the Lord / to prepare straight paths for him, / Giving his people a knowledge of salvation / in freedom from their sins" (Luke 1:76-77). We, too, are to hear and heed this prayer as we prepare the way of the Lord not only in our own hearts but in the hearts of those whom we meet.

Meditation: What is God saying to you this Advent? In what ways do you demonstrate that you truly hear the word of God?

Prayer: Loving and demanding God, you hold us accountable for the messages sent to us through the prophet and your great law of love. Open our ears to your wisdom and strengthen our hearts with your courage. May we put into practice your plan of salvation by acting justly in all our transactions, by loving tenderly all of our brothers and sisters, by walking in faith and hope all the days of our life. Send your Spirit of fidelity into our souls that we may be truly a people made your own. Grant this through Jesus, our great prophet and redeemer and friend. Amen.

Wisdom

Mass: Isa 48:17-19; Matt 11:16-19

Scripture:
   Jesus said to the crowds:
   "Yet time will prove where wisdom lies." (Matt 11:19)

Reflection: Given the explosion of knowledge and vast pluralism of our culture it is not surprising that we can become muddled. Confusion reigns. What are we to believe? How are we to act? What is the meaning of life? From all sides a variety of voices cry out seeking our attention. Where can we find true wisdom?

   Jesus is our master teacher. By using comparisons (analogies) he cuts through the seeming complexity of life down to its bare bones. Wisdom is responding appropriately to the grace of the moment. It is doing what is pleasing to God here and now. If a tune is played, we are to dance. If a dirge is heard, we are to wail and mourn. It's as simple and complex as that. Children for the most part do respond to the moment; we, adults, "far older and wiser (?) than they," think we are smarter but our actions betray the claim.

   Jesus is neither mad nor self-indulgent. When called to be in the penitential mood, he refrains from eating and drinking. When he goes to Cana for a wedding, he enjoys the food and wine. When meeting tax collectors and those outside the law, he greets them as brothers and sisters of a common Father. Much wisdom here! Indeed, wisdom that time proves accurate and sound.

Meditation: Where do you go for wisdom? What wisdom have you passed on to your friends, children, peers?

Prayer: Come, O Spirit of Wisdom. Come into our minds and hearts that we may know what is truly pleasing to you. Breathe on us your knowledge and understanding so that we may respond appropriately to the joys and sorrows of life. May we dance at our wedding feasts; may we weep at the loss of dear friends. May Jesus, your Wisdom, guide us to the kingdom of peace. To do your will is true wisdom; to follow your law is supreme grace. Come, O Spirit of Wisdom, come!

Questions

Mass: Sir 48:1-4, 9-11; Matt 17:10-13

Scripture:
As they were coming down the mountainside,
the disciples put this question to Jesus: . . . . (Matt 17:10)

Reflection: The three big questions in life center around identity, destiny, and morality: "Who am I?" "Where am I going?" "How do I get there?" (And, for some of us, a fourth question: "What time is recess?") We all search for meaning so that we can make sense of this complex life. Psychologists tell us that meaninglessness is sickness. Without answers to the basic questions we become paralyzed.

God sends us prophets to address life's large questions. Elijah and John the Baptist, through their teaching and example, point the way to God. Jesus himself, *the* prophet, proclaims the love and mercy of God that offers us a vision of what life is all about. Was the poet William Blake correct when he wrote: "And we are put on earth a little space / That we may learn to bear the beams of love"? Love is the ultimate answer to all life's questions.

St. Ignatius, a prophet in his own day, held that we came from God, we belong to God, and we are all going back to God. If we accept this proposition as true, then we come to know that we are God's beloved sons and daughters; that our destiny is one of getting back to God from whence we came; that life is one of discipleship, belonging to God with our whole mind, our whole heart, and our whole soul. We do well this Advent to ascend the mountainside and ask the Lord our favorite questions.

Meditation: What are the three or four questions that have remained with you over the years? Where do you go for answers to life's questions?

Prayer: Lord Jesus, we have so many questions. We sit at your feet in prayer seeking to know what this journey is all about. Help us to ask the right, the real questions. Open our hearts to see how your very life is a life of "answers." May we be authentic; may we realize in action what you ask of us. We are a pilgrim people and we often lose our way. May we seek the answers to our questions not in the back of some book but in the place called Bethlehem and Calvary. By participating in your life our questions will find resolution. Be with us, Lord, this day. Amen.

THIRD WEEK OF ADVENT

The Glory of the Lord

Mass: Isa 35:1-6, 10; Jas 5:7-10; Matt 11:2-11

Scripture:
Jesus said to them:
> "Go back and report to John what you hear and see: the
> blind
> recover their sight, cripples walk, lepers are cured, the
> deaf hear,
> dead men are raised to life, and the poor have the good
> news
> preached to them. Blest is the man who finds no stumbling
> block
> in me." (Matt 11:4-6)

Reflection: Isaiah, the prophet, made a prediction that we would one day see "the glory of the Lord, the splendor of our God." He goes on to say that the blind will see, the deaf will hear, the lame will leap, and the dumb will speak and sing. In Jesus, that glory has become manifest and, in Jesus, we see the splendor of the Father and the power of the Holy Spirit.

How was this message received by John the Baptist who was in the darkness of prison? Surely he knew that the end was near. His mission had been accomplished by his preparing the way for Jesus and by preaching repentance of sins. Jesus was impressed by his cousin for John was more than a prophet. Now John would experience God's glory through the gateway of death.

In the letter of James we are reminded that the prophets have been for us models of how to be patient and embrace hardships. Jesus and John are two primary examples of how we are to live our lives. They were focused on the Father's will and surrendered to his sway. For many, the prophets were stumbling blocks but not for those with eyes of faith.

Meditation: What do you understand by the "glory" of God? What do you learn from the examples of the prophets?

Prayer: God of glory and splendor, you have revealed the radiance of your light and love in Jesus our Lord. Help us to imitate your Son by radiating your glory to those we meet. Help us to reveal through our words and deeds the mystery and extravagance of your love. By so doing, we will truly be Advent people, preparing your way. Grant this through Jesus your Son in the power of the Holy Spirit. Amen.

December 13: Monday of the Third Week of Advent

A Whole New Life

Mass: Num 24:2-7, 15-17; Matt 21:23-27

Scripture:
   Jesus answered:
   "I too will ask a question . . . .
   What was the origin of John's baptism?
   Was it divine or human?" (Matt 21:24-25)

Reflection: In his book *Against the Infinite Horizons* (New York: Crossroad, 1996), Fr. Ronald Rolheiser comments: "To submit to love is to be baptized" (173). God's love is made present and manifest in Jesus and in a very special way through our sacramental life. When we are baptized, we plunge into the mystery of God's love and mercy. And later in life, when we again and again submit to the mystery of love we continue to be baptized.

   John the Baptist knew himself to be loved. This began in his mother's womb as Elizabeth rejoiced in God's gift of life. The Baptist experienced his father's love as Zechariah sang this canticle and foretold his son's mission of preparing the way of the Lord. Later in life when John watched the ministry of Jesus, he knew himself loved by the Messiah. John's baptism was divine because God is love and submitting to the grace of love is to plunge into God's life.

When we were baptized, our parents presented us to the Church, this community of faith and love. The experience of being loved reached far beyond the walls of our home into the universal Church. Our baptism was divine because it stemmed all the way back to Jesus and the apostles. We were sealed with the Holy Spirit and given a baptismal robe to be carried spotless through life. We were given a candle and challenged to be a light unto others. While using so many human symbols and signs, we received divine life. That life, during this Advent season, is to grow to even fuller maturity.

Meditation: What is your understanding of baptism? In what sense are we "being baptized" continuously throughout our lives?

Prayer: God of life, you plunge us into the baptismal waters of grace. What a miracle that we can participate in your very life through the mystery of Jesus. You have given us a whole new life, far beyond our natural existence. The origin of our baptism is divine; the destiny of our baptism is eternal life. Keep us mindful of our baptismal commitments. Keep our baptismal candle burning bright that we might attract others to the life of grace. Grant this through Jesus, your Son and our Lord. Amen.

The Kingdom

Mass: Zep 3:1-2, 9-13; Matt 21:28-32

Scripture:
Jesus said to them,
"Let me make it clear that tax collectors and prostitutes
are entering the kingdom of God before you." (Matt 21:31)

Reflection: To walk the talk (authenticity) is a significant part of our faith life. If we truly believe and repent for our sins, then we follow the way of the Lord, the path of holiness. Walking the talk means that we enter the kingdom of God, for by doing what God asks of us we come under the reign of God.

The Gospel "case" is quite clear. The son who did what the father wanted performed deeds. Speech was not sufficient; the test was in the doing (orthopraxis). Here is a faith that flows into action. Many who do not profess the Christian creed (à la tax collectors and prostitutes) may well be doing the work of the kingdom that we are unaware of. In the Acts of the Apostles Peter shouts out an insight about there being no partiality in God. In fact, whoever fears God and does what is good is pleasing to the Lord. Reverential fear and the doing of good give us access to the kingdom.

Jesus tells us that John preached the way of holiness. Holiness, within our Catholic tradition, is the perfection of love. What God wants of us is that we be a loving community, deeply concerned about the well-being of all our brothers and sisters. We are sent into the vineyard not to make money and achieve fame, but to serve those in need. The path of holiness is following Jesus in a life of dedicated service. If our faith is authentic, then our love will be sincere. And, even more, our hope of eternal life will be built on a firm foundation.

Meditation: How do we enter and remain in the kingdom of God? What do you understand by "the way of holiness"?

Prayer: Lord Jesus, you came to establish the reign of God in the minds and hearts of people. You come during this season of Advent in word and sacrament so that we too might repent and believe, that we too might walk the path of holiness. Empower us to do what your Father wants. Give us deep faith that we might say yes to the coming of your kingdom. As the Christmas mystery approaches, may we go out in the vineyard and work hard in helping others see your love and mercy. Grant this through the power of your Spirit. Amen.

December 15: Wednesday of the Third Week of Advent

Seeking

Mass: Isa 45:6-8, 18, 21-25; Luke 7:18-23

Scripture:
   Summoning two of his disciples, John sent them to ask
   the Lord, "Are you 'He who is to come' or are we
   to expect someone else?" (Luke 7:18)

Reflection: One of the great mystics of the Church, St. John
of the Cross, maintained that even though we seek God,
much more is God seeking us. That is why he sent Jesus
into the world: that we might be found and saved. He is indeed the one who is to come and there is no need to seek
further.

   Yet, strange to say, many people have found in Jesus a
stumbling block. How is it possible, they ask, that God can
take on our human nature and still remain divine? Why
would the incarnate God be so concerned about the poor
and wounded of the world? And, the very last straw, how
could the Messiah wind up being nailed to a cross, hung
between common thieves?

   In searching out and identifying the Savior of the world,
we need look nowhere else than into the eyes of Jesus. Here
we find the compassion of our infinite God; here we find
forgiveness of all our sins; here we find the desire to restore
everyone to the fullness of life. It is in the presence of this

divine gaze that our joy and peace reside, and no place else. John the Baptist knew this, for he, like Jesus, was willing to give his life in doing the Father's will.

Meditation: What are you looking for? In whom (or what) do you find salvation?

Prayer: Generous God, you sent your Son into our wounded world to teach and heal, to forgive and bring you glory. May we find in Jesus no stumbling block but only our redeemer and friend. May we not look for anyone else or anything else to satisfy our infinite longings. And once having found him in word and sacrament, send us forth to tell others what we have seen and heard and experienced. We ask this through the power of the Holy Spirit. Amen.

Prophet

Mass: Isa 54:1-10; Luke 7:24-30

Scripture:
Jesus began to speak about him [John the Baptist]
to the crowds . . . "Then what did you go out to see—
a prophet? He is that, I assure you, and something more."
(Luke 7: 24b, 26)

Reflection: In his book *The Prophetic Imagination,* the Scripture scholar Walter Bruggemann states that a prophet is one who criticizes and one who energizes. The criticism of the prophets is directed to the injustices and lies of the world; the energizing is directed to doing God's will and bringing about God's reign.

John the Baptist was not afraid to criticize the culture of his day. John saw sin for what it was, the breaking of relationships and God's law. His call was one of repentance, a turning from sin to new life. John's criticism of Herod eventually led to his death. So committed was John to the truth that he was willing to give his life for it. Much courage was needed here.

But Jesus tells us that John was even more than a prophet. In the Baptist we find a special messenger who announced the coming of the Savior of the world. John prepared for this coming by proclaiming the forgiveness of sin. The baptism that he performed led to the conversion of many individuals. Those who did not submit to these life-giving waters remained in darkness and sin, unaffected by the prophetic ministry.

Meditation: Who are the prophets that have spoken to you of God? In saying that John was more than a prophet, what did Jesus mean? In what way are you a prophet?

Prayer: Lord Jesus, you continue to come to us in so many ways: through the sacraments, through the community, through the Scriptures, and through so many prophets. During the season of Advent, the prophet Isaiah has spoken of God's concern. During this season of Advent, the prophet John the Baptist has spoken of you and your ministry. Open our ears and hearts to their message. Give us the courage we need to speak the truth and draw us to you. We ask this in your name. Amen.

Family Tree

Mass: Gen 49:2, 8-10; Matt 1:1-17

Scripture:
  A family record of Jesus Christ, son of David,
  son of Abraham. (Matt 1:1)

Reflection: Most families have a skeleton or two in their closet, and they hope that they stay there. If we have an uncle who is in prison for murder or a sister who is a prostitute or a grandparent convicted of fraud or a son guilt of adultery—well, we prefer that the newspapers do not get hold of these facts.

Jesus had in his genealogy individuals who sinned grievously. One example will do: the great King David. Here was a leader who was guilty of adultery and murder. David slept with his general's wife and then had Uriah killed. Jesus came from this lineage. Jesus came to embrace the human condition and to redeem it from the inside. Purists would prefer that Jesus' family tree were impeccable. Such was not the case. Jesus rubbed his nose in the messiness of human history.

As we approach the Christmas mystery we begin to sing out the first "O" Antiphon: "Wisdom of our God Most High, guiding creation with power and love: teach us to walk in the paths of knowledge." God's wisdom is expressed in the mystery of the Incarnation, the divine becoming incarnate in human history, a history filled with darkness and chaos. Jesus breaks in with power and love to do the creative work of redemption and to teach us to walk in the paths of knowledge and peace. How grateful we should be for so condescending a God.

Meditation: What impression does the genealogy of Jesus make on you? What are some of the moments of grace that stand out in your own family tree?

Prayer: God of Abraham, God of David, help us to embrace our history and to discover how your grace has been working throughout the ages. We are a wounded people in need of your saving help. Forgive us our sins and fill us with the Spirit of your mercy and love. May compassion and not judgment govern our hearts. We give you thanks for coming to us in our messy history and taking on our limitations and frailness. You know us from the inside and for this we give you praise and thanks. Amen.

December 18: Saturday of the Third Week of Advent

Joseph's Annunciation

Mass: Jer 23:5-8; Matt 1:18-25

Scripture:
  . . . suddenly the angel of the Lord appeared in a dream
  and said to him: "Joseph, son of David, have no fear about
  taking Mary as your wife." (Matt 1:20)

Reflection: Both Mary and Joseph experienced God's special revelation. Both of them had to struggle with fear and
ignorance as God broke into their lives with special requests. Both Joseph and Mary were told of the action of the
Holy Spirit, an event that transformed their lives and
world history. We see in them people of deep faith and
trust.

  During this season of Advent, we too are called to be
open to the Lord's visitation. What happened in the lives of
Joseph and Mary, of Zechariah and Elizabeth, of Augustine
and Francis, can happen to us if we are properly disposed.
"God is with us," this God we call Emmanuel, and desires
that through the faith community God's presence will be
not only present but manifest. Each of us is to conceive
God's word in our souls and, through the power of the
Holy Spirit, bring that word to fruition.

  Advent is about the coming of Jesus into history. As we
prepare our hearts daily for the great Christmas mystery,

we do well to beg God to transform our fears and ignorance into courage and knowledge. With the coming of Jesus all is made new. To the extent that we allow Jesus to have sway in our hearts, the world too will be transformed. Advent holds the possibility of a social revolution because once the power of the Spirit is released, the old reign of sin will be broken.

Meditation: In what ways are the annunciation events to Joseph and Mary similar? How does the Holy Spirit come to you in moments of fear and unknowing?

Prayer: Spirit of the living God, descend upon us in this Advent season. So many fears dominate our lives; so much ignorance blocks us from knowing your ways. Come to us with wisdom and courage that we might listen to the angels that speak your truth. May we, like Joseph, be attentive to our dreams and come to believe that you are truly with us. Come, Holy Spirit, come! Amen.

FOURTH WEEK OF ADVENT

December 19: Fourth Sunday of Advent

Ongoing Revelation

Mass: Isa 7:10-14; Rom 1:1-7; Matt 1:18-24

Scripture:
"Joseph, son of David, have no fear about taking Mary as your wife. It is by the Holy Spirit that she has conceived this child. She is to have a son and you are to name him Jesus because he will save his people from their sins."
(Matt 1:20-21)

Reflection: Members of the house of David had a special relationship with God. Ahaz was the recipient of God's revelation as was Joseph, both members of the house of David. More, the message was essentially the same: a son would be born of Mary, a son who would bring to the world the message of salvation, the message that God is with us. Both Ahaz and Joseph had some difficulty in accepting the message but in the end they got it.

St. Paul too speaks of David and instructs us that Jesus, the Son of God, descended from the Davidic line. The message here is clear and strong: Jesus is one of us. The mystery of the Incarnation, God-become-man, gives us blessed assurance that our God knows the human condition from the inside. David had his struggles: murder, adultery, and misuse of power. Yet he was God's chosen one and through him the Messiah would come.

Let us not forget Mary and the Holy Spirit. Mary said yes to God; the Holy Spirit filled her being to the brim. Through a life of obedience and self-giving, Mary would model for us what the Church is to be. By her surrender to God's will, Mary points us to the source of peace and joy. We should have no fear of allowing Jesus to be conceived in us.

Meditation: What revelations has the Lord given to you? In what ways has Jesus saved you from your sins?

Prayer: Loving God, like Ahaz we sometimes weary you in not understanding your plan for us. Like Joseph, we too are often afraid to take Jesus into our hearts lest he ask too much. Help us to be like Mary, open and obedient, generous and hospitable. Mary knew how difficult life could be. Through her intercession may we have no fear in saying yes to whatever you ask of us.

December 20: Monday of the Fourth Week of Advent

Invasions of Grace

Mass: Isa 7:10-14; Luke 1:26-38

Scripture:
   The angel answered her: "The Holy Spirit will
   come upon you and the power of the Most High
   will overshadow you." (Luke 1:35)

Reflection: The poet Gerard Manley Hopkins (1844–1889) concludes his famous sonnet "God's Grandeur" with these lines: "Because the Holy Ghost over the bent / World broods with warm breast and with ah! bright wings." Hopkins's verse expresses a hovering, providential God, brooding over all creation. The challenge for creation is twofold: to be aware and to be open. Mary, the mother of Jesus, is our paradigm. She believed in God's presence and said yes to the divine invitation.

Jessica Powers (1905–1988), a Carmelite versifier, made the claim that to live with the Spirit is to be both a listener and a lover. The power of the Most High attunes us to the divine plan; more, that same God empowers us to respond in love. Mary was a listener and a lover, par excellence. She aligned her will to God and responded by total self-giving.

The poet George Herbert was conscious of the Holy Spirit breaking into history, his own and the world's. He writes in the last stanza of "Matins": "Teach me thy love to know; / That this new light, which now I see, / May both the work and workman show: / Then by a sunbeam I will climb to thee." God's invading light and love is the Holy Spirit in action. We need but catch a single sunbeam—a deed of kindness, a word of forgiveness, a look of compassion—to know the presence of God in our lives. Mary was taught how to love and see. Daily she climbed into the Lord's presence because the Holy Spirit was upon her.

Meditation: What is your experience of the coming of the Holy Spirit in your life? How has God's presence been manifest on your journey?

Prayer: God of power and love, you long to share your life with us. Open our minds and hearts to your visitations. Do not let our fear or ignorance impede your invasions of grace. Like Mary, give us trust and confidence in your ways, however unknown. Let us not seek security in anything or anyone but you. Come, Holy Spirit, come.

December 21: Tuesday of the Fourth Week of Advent

Advent Joy

Mass: Cant 2:8-14 or Zeph 3:14-18; Luke 1:39-45

Scripture:
"Blessed are you among women and blessed
is the fruit of your womb. But who am I that
the mother of my Lord should come to me?" (Luke 1:42-43)

Reflection: One of the joyful mysteries of the Rosary is the Visitation. This blessed moment tells of a double visitation: Mary greeting Elizabeth, Jesus and John encountering one another though still in the wombs of their mothers. The keynote of this mystery is joy: that experiential knowledge that something good is happening to and in us.

Advent is a season of joy. Jesus comes to all of us in word and sacrament, in community and daily experience. Something should stir within us as we are exposed to God's light and love and life. This visitation is often incarnate through others: a phone call of concern from a friend, an unexpected visit from a long-lost classmate, the restoration of health, an invitation to embrace a cross that might well transform our lives. God is on the move and just as Mary journeyed to see her cousin Elizabeth, God journeys into our lives on a daily basis.

Elizabeth struggled to receive Mary and to understand the import of the visitation. Her struggle dealt with unworthiness. "But who am I . . .?" We are all in that identical situation. None of us is worthy to house our God and yet God has nowhere else to go. More, regardless of our sins and failures, God longs to be at the center of our lives. Herein is our joy: God's love visiting us today, here and now. No excuses will be accepted. Joy will win out.

Meditation: Is joy a central experience in your life? What is the relationship between "presence" and joy?

Prayer: God of joy and hope, you come to us in our weakness and discouragement. Your visitations are not limited to a particular season of the year. No, you are coming to us today, in the here and now. Through Elizabeth's intercession may we be open to your coming; through the prayers of Mary, may we say yes to your will. Fill us with your hope and joy. Make us good disciples of your Son Jesus. Amen.

Singing Our Gratitude

Mass: 1 Sam 1:24-28; Luke 1:46-56

Scripture:
Mary said:
> "My being proclaims the greatness of the Lord,
>   my spirit finds joy in God my savior,
> For he has looked upon his servant in her lowliness;
>   all ages to come shall call me blessed." (Luke 1:46-48)

Reflection: When gifted, the healthy person gives thanks. Hannah was gifted with a son named Samuel; Mary was gifted with a son named Jesus. Both women turned to the Lord in profound gratitude for the gift of life given to them. Both women realized that God had looked upon them in love and both responded with appropriate praise.

Advent is a liturgical season in which the Church tries to remind us, through word and sacrament, that all of us are looked upon with love. Everything that we are and have is ultimately God's grace. Too seldom are we aware of this; too seldom do we turn with our whole being to the living and true God to give thanks and praise. No wonder, then, that we do not experience the blessedness that filled the soul of Hannah and Mary.

The God known by Hannah and Mary was a giving, generous God. No need was too large or too small to be addressed. Here is a God who does great things for us and small as well. This God is faithful to promises and is mindful of his mercy. It is in the mystery of the Incarnation that we come to know the fulfillment of divine promises and to experience the power of divine mercy.

Meditation: Is gratitude a virtue that dominates your life? What image of God fills your soul?

Prayer: God of mercy and generosity, you came to Hannah and Mary in their deepest need. Through them you deepened your life on earth. Come to us during this season of Advent that we too might be instruments of your praise. Fill our hearts with gratitude for all that you have done for us. May our being proclaim your greatness and our hearts love you forever. Amen.

December 23: Thursday of the Fourth Week of Advent

God's Fire and Lye

Mass: Mal 3:1-4, 23-24; Luke 1:57-66

Scripture:
When they assembled for the circumcision of the child on the eighth day, they intended to name him after his father Zechariah. At this his mother intervened, saying,

"No, he is to be called John." (Luke 1:59-60)

Reflection: The refiner's fire and the fuller's lye are dangerous things. Their work of refining and purifying are experienced as painful and even destructive. Yet all of us are in need of cleansing and God sends into the world prophets to do that work. As we near the Christmas mystery we hear about two prophets who helped to prepare the way of the Lord.

One is John the Baptist, the cousin of Jesus. The name John signifies "Yahweh has shown favor." Already at his birth powerful things are happening. A woman exercises her power in naming her child. A father, silenced because of a lack of faith, now begins to speak again and does so by praising God. The neighbors and relatives are astounded at the events and are forced to ask questions about the future of this child and about the working of divine providence.

The refrain from the responsorial psalm instructs us: "Lift up your heads and see; your redemption is near at hand." With the eyes of faith we see in Elijah and John how God prepares the human heart to the workings of grace. But these are human prophets only. In Jesus, we see our redemption, the forgiveness of our sins. Herein lies our hope. It is good to store all these things in our Advent hearts.

Meditation: What is your experience of prophetic fire and lye? How has God purified you over your Christian journey? What are the things you store up in your heart?

Prayer: God of wind and fire, continue to send into our lives prophets of truth. Often we live the lie and thus lose our freedom. Through Jesus and the prophets of old you call us into the light of your love. Though this is painfully purifying, we are given new life and new freedoms. Speak again and again your purifying word. And then our hearts will be filled with memories of your mercy and love.

Zechariah's Song

Mass: 2 Sam 7:1-5, 8-12, 14, 16; Luke 1:67-79

Scripture:
Zechariah, the father of John, filled with the Holy Spirit, uttered this prophecy:
   "Blessed be the Lord the God of Israel
   because he has visited and ransomed his people."
      (Luke 1:67-68)

Reflection: During these days before Christmas we hear many different people singing the praises of God: Hannah, Mary, Elizabeth, and now Zechariah. Here is a proud father's song flowing out of a deep faith in God's redemptive love. Zechariah knew his history. God made promises in ancient days through the prophets and now those promises were being realized. And it was Zechariah's own son, John, who would be an instrument in preparing the way for Jesus, our Redeemer.

Songs carry our theology. The lyrics tell us who God is and what we are about. In this canticle we learn that God remembers his covenant, that our enemies will be overcome, that we are to live in holiness and righteousness all our days, that salvation comes through the forgiveness of our sins, that God visits us with his mercy and guides our feet into the way of peace. As we hum this hymn we grow in our faith; as we live this hymn we express God's grace.

This God spoken of by Zechariah is the same God spoken of by Nathan, a prophet of old. Nathan informs David, the king of Israel, that God's providential love has been active in his life. For it was God who pastured and cared for him and his people; it was God who gives rest from one's enemies; it is God who is always with us. Our God is a creative, redeeming, and sanctifying God through all the ages.

Meditation: What hymns and songs sustain your faith journey? What do you understand by: "To sing well, is to pray twice"?

Prayer: God of song and dance, help us to sing your praises. Like Zechariah, may we be aware of your healing, redemptive love. Our enemies are many, both within and without. It is only in Jesus that we are set free from our sins. It is only in Jesus that holiness becomes a possibility. Stir our hearts to sing your praise. Fill our souls with deep faith and everlasting love. Come, Holy Spirit, come. Amen.

CHRISTMAS AND DAYS
WITHIN ITS OCTAVE

Vigil Mass: Jesus' Family Tree

Mass: Isa 62:1-5; Acts 13:16-17, 22-25; Matt 1:1-25 or 1:18-25

Scripture:
Jacob was the father of Joseph the husband of Mary.
It was of her that Jesus who is called the Messiah was
  born. (Matt 1:16)

Reflection: Our family tree is revelatory. We see there our parents, grandparents, great-grandparents, and on and on. Jesus, born of Mary, belongs to the history of the Jewish people. We see on the family tree saints and sinners, kings and adulterers, wise people and murderers. Jesus took on all of human history and by so doing brought to it the grace of redemption.

Joseph is a part of that history. He was, as God's word tells us, an upright man. More, he was open to God's will. We hear how, through a dream, Joseph received assurance that the child to be born was truly Emmanuel, "God with us." In response, Joseph took Mary into his home and into his heart and remained forever faithful.

And what went on in the heart of Mary? We know from the Annunciation story that she had to deal with fear and ignorance. But Mary too was upright and holy, believing that the things God would do for her were in accord with his will. Mary's confusion turned to joy because of her faith. She bore a son and they named him Jesus. And in that moment all of history was radically changed.

Meditation: How does God speak to you? In dreams? In nature? In Scripture? In looking at your family tree, how has God been present to your ancestors?

Prayer: Lord Jesus, son of Mary, send your Spirit of wisdom into our lives. Help us to see more clearly who you are and what you have done for our salvation. We are grateful for the great mystery of your Nativity. We marvel at the faith of Joseph and Mary and their response to your presence. May we truly believe that you are God with us. May we commit ourselves to taking you into our homes and sharing you with others. Amen.

Mass at Midnight: Fear Nothing

Mass: Isa 9:1-6; Titus 2:11-14; Luke 2:1-14

Scripture:
The angel said to them [the shepherds]:
  "You have nothing to fear! I come to proclaim
  good news to you—tidings of great joy to be shared
  by the whole people. This day in David's city a
  savior has been born to you, the Messiah and Lord."
    (Luke 2:10-11)

Reflection: It would seem that shepherds have much to fear: the darkness of night, the threat of wolves attacking the flock, low wages making life precarious, and the list goes on. So easily we become trapped and oppressed by worry and anxiety. The news is not good and life becomes heavy.

It is in the center of our fears and tribulation that God breaks into our lives. The good news is that God is with us, that God not only creates but loves us, that God is our savior and friend. What tidings of great joy we have here. And all of this is manifest in the birth of a baby, in the mystery of the Nativity of our Lord. Jesus is the one who saves us and frees us from sin and fear. Jesus is the Messiah, the liberator who conquers death and sin.

The shepherds received a double message on that sacred night. They not only heard about the birth of the Messiah, but they also heard "Glory to God in high heaven, peace on earth to those on whom his favor rests" (Luke 2:14). Good news leads to glad tidings that in turn leads to glory. In Jesus we see the radiance and splendor of God. In Jesus we find our peace and are reconciled once and for all.

Meditation: How do you deal with your fears? How does Jesus free you from worry and give you peace?

Prayer: Angels of God, come to us in our darkness. We have so many fears and anxieties. Help us to hear the glad tidings of Jesus; lead us into that peace which the world cannot give. May our lives glorify God by bearing much fruit. May the gift of faith help us to trust that the birth of Jesus is our only and deepest hope. Amen.

Mass at Dawn: Treasuring and Reflecting

Mass: Isa 62: 11-12; Titus 3:4-7; Luke 2:15-20

Scripture:

Mary treasured all these things and reflected on them in her heart. The shepherds returned, glorifying and praising God for all they had heard and seen, in accord with what has been told them. (Luke 2:19-20)

Reflection: There are certain experiences to be treasured and reflected upon often. One of those is the birth of one's child. What a miracle here! Mary, the mother of Jesus and the mother of the Church, treasured her greatest gift: her son Jesus. And she contemplated his person and life deeply within her heart. Treasuring and reflecting became a way of life that led to love and peace.

The shepherds too treasured and reflected. They had seen and heard some marvelous things, things like the birth of the Messiah and peace coming to the earth and the uselessness of fear. How could they not glorify and praise God for such wonderful happenings?

Our challenge this Christmas Day is also to treasure and reflect upon things that really matter. Not the gifts exchanged on the feast of Christmas but the love that underlies this great mystery of the birth of Jesus. Not to treasure this life of grace and not to see its meaning and implications in our lives is to fail in our universal vocation: to be the recipients of God's love and mercy and to share these gifts with others.

Meditation: What do you treasure? What do you spend your time reflecting upon? What goes on in the deepest recesses of your heart?

Prayer: Mary, mother of Jesus, intercede for us on this holy feast. Your life was one of reverent cherishing and diligent reflection. Pray that we too may hold dear the mystery of Jesus within us; pray that we may understand the meaning of our call to discipleship. Then, with the angels, we too will glorify and praise God for all that he has done and is doing in our lives. Amen.

Mass During the Day: God's Enduring Love

Mass: Isa 52:7-10; Heb 1:1-6; John 1-18 or 1:1-5, 9-14

Scripture:
  The Word became flesh
  and made his dwelling among us,
  and we have seen his glory:
  the glory of an only Son coming from the Father,
  filled with enduring love. (John 1:14)

Reflection: It is in the mysteries of the Incarnation and Nativity of our Lord that we are given the glory of God. Our finite minds and hearts struggle to grasp and cherish the reality of an infinite and transcendent God breaking into history through flesh and blood, indeed a stumbling block and a scandal to so many.

Yet we witness here the humility of God. In the divine self-emptying *(kenosis)* we come to know the extravagance of God's love, God's enduring love. Creation is not enough. Incarnation must follow to convince us that our Triune God is truly with and in us. Unfortunately we are slow learners and so, year after year, the mysteries of our faith are presented to us that we might eventually "get it." But even time is not enough; we will need eternity in our pursuit of divine wisdom.

God's glory—"the glory of an only Son"—turns our conventional wisdom upside down. Glory in the form of poverty? Glory coming through suffering and death? Glory expressing love through the Incarnation? God's wisdom is not ours. We need the gift of faith to begin to have even an initial understanding of this Christmas event. May the gift be under everyone's tree.

Meditation: What do you understand by the glory of God? How have you experienced God's enduring love?

Prayer: Jesus, Word made flesh, open our eyes to the wonder of your Father's enduring love. That is, open our eyes to you. You are the glory of the Father and true brother to us. We thank you for coming among us to experience our lives from the inside. May we, this day, experience your glory and love; may we in turn become love incarnate for others, especially for those who have so little. Come, Lord Jesus, come. Amen.

December 26: Feast of the Holy Family

The Family—The Domestic Church

Mass: Sir 3:2-6, 12-14; Col 3:12-21; Matt 2:13-15, 19-23

Scripture:
After the astrologers had left, the angel of the Lord suddenly appeared in a dream to Joseph with the command:
"Get up, take the child and his mother,
and flee to Egypt" (Matt 2:13).

Reflection: The novelist Jon Hassler, in an autobiographical piece, begins by stating that he had the "great, good fortune" of being born into a loving family. Indeed, what a great, glorious, marvelous fortune that is. To be raised in a loving, caring environment is a blessing so momentous that we falter to find words to describe it in any adequate way.

The Holy Family—Joseph, Mary, and Jesus—is a model for all of our homes. Joseph's protection and care, Mary's love and constant self-giving, and Jesus' gracious obedience gives us an ideal and vision of what a healthy community looks like. And this family was not without its danger and tribulations. At birth, trouble was brooding as Herod sought to kill the newborn. Later in life, Jesus experienced rejection and condemnation, but Mary, his mother, stood by him all the way to the cross. Loving families stick together in all seasons.

In a culture of radical individualism, community in all its forms is threatened, and one of those communities is the family. Living together demands sacrifice, self-forgetfulness, and a deep sense of the common good. If our families are to be holy, that is, truly loving, then we must take on the qualities of the Holy Family if we are to achieve peace and joy. To the extent that we listen to the Lord, as he sends angels or opportunities or transforming events, we will be able to know that peace and joy that is beyond all understanding. This is the peace and joy that Joseph and Mary knew as they raised the Christ child.

Meditation: What is your relationship to your family of origin? What qualities do you bring to the human family?

Prayer: On this feast of the Holy Family, we ask you, Joseph, Mary, and Jesus, to teach us how to care and share with one another. Too often we go our own way, not heeding the voice of God to live out a rich and deep solidarity. Through your intercession may we come to know that God is Father of us all and we are sisters and brothers to one another. May the Holy Spirit transform our world into one huge family, all participants building the kingdom of God. Grant this, loving Father, in your good time. Amen.

Gospel Urgency

Mass: 1 John 1:1-4; John 20:2-8

Scripture:
On the first day of the week Mary Magdalene ran off to Simon Peter and the other disciple (the one Jesus loved) and told them:
> "The Lord has been taken from the tomb! We do not know where they have put him!" (John 20:2)

Reflection: One of the scenes that all of us remember from 9/11 as the Twin Towers in New York began to fall was people running for their lives away from the tragedy. It was, indeed, a matter of life or death. The running was an obvious sign of the urgency of the matter.

In our Gospel today we see people running. Mary Magdalene ran to Peter and the other disciples; then Peter and the beloved disciple ran to the tomb. Urgency, life and death, tragedy. There is no time to waste when it comes to a matter of the Christian life. Faith demands that we hurry to find our Savior and leave behind everything that would impede us from the search. The time is now; the day of discipleship is here.

The expression "Tomorrow may be too late" is worth pondering. Putting things off (the big word here is procrastination) is most dangerous for the spiritual life. Tomorrow may never come. The needs of today demand our immediate response if at all possible. We must run to meet our Lord in the suffering and sick, in the lonely and the discouraged, in the alienated and marginalized. Mary Magdalene and the disciples have given us a good example.

Meditation: What is your sense of urgency regarding your Christian life? Is procrastination a major problem in your life?

Prayer: Lord Jesus, you are risen and living among us. Help us to hurry to find you in those around us. Do not let us postpone or delay our response to your call. Today is indeed the day of our salvation. Send your Spirit into our lives so that, filled with your energy and enthusiasm, we may accomplish the work you have given us to do. We ask this through the intercession of Mary Magdalene and your beloved disciples. Amen.

December 28: Feast of the Holy Innocents, Martyrs

A Grief Observed and Felt

Mass: 1 John 1:5–2:2; Matt 2:13-18

Scripture:
What was said through Jeremiah the prophet was then fulfilled:
> "A cry was heard at Ramah,
> sobbing and loud lamentation:
> Rachel bewailing her children;
> no comfort for her, since they are no more"
> (Matt 2:17-18).

Reflection: In a small volume, *A Grief Observed*, the Christian writer C. S. Lewis wrote about the feelings and thoughts he had when his wife of three years died of cancer. Lewis' grief was deep and passionate just like his love for his wife. Anger, fear, confusion, doubt were all part of Lewis's grieving process.

We can well imagine the pain and grief that tore through the villages as Herod and his men killed innocent babies. Lamentation and sobbing indeed filled Ramah and no comfort seemed to lessen the sorrow. Jesus was born into this violent and cruel world to bring it God's peace and forgiveness. Even as an infant the child Jesus was surrounded by the brutality of certain individuals.

This Christmas season is filled with birth and death. Jesus born in poverty, Stephen martyred, the Holy Innocents killed. Already we are sensing the paschal mystery that underlies our Christian existence. Just as Jesus participated in our life and death, so we too are to participate in his and come to the glory of the resurrection. Death has lost its sting in the mystery of the God-made-man.

Meditation: What is the connection between life and death for you? How do you deal with your grief and the grief of others?

Prayer: God of the living and the dead, send your Spirit upon our world. Help us to respect all life, especially the lives of those who are most vulnerable. Put an end to our brutality and insensitivity. Make us instruments of your peace and make us agents of your reconciliation. Draw us deeply into the paschal mystery of your Son so that all fear will banish. Grant this through the intercession of the Holy Innocents. Amen.

A Sword of Sorrow

Mass: 1 John 2:3-11; Luke 2:22-35

Scripture:
Simeon blessed them and said to Mary his mother:
> "This child is destined to be the downfall and the rise
> of many in Israel, a sign that will be opposed—and you
> yourself shall be pierced with a sword—so that the
> thoughts of many hearts may be laid bare." (Luke 2:34-35)

Reflection: We know just a few things about Simeon—he
was just, he was pious, and the Holy Spirit was upon him.
He also offered a blessing upon the infant Jesus and Mary
and Joseph. Simeon saw in this experience the glory of God
and now he was ready to die. Down through the centuries
Simeon has been a witness to salvation in Jesus.

We know just a few things about Mary—she was a
woman of deep faith, the mother of Jesus, and someone
who would suffer deeply. In fact, a sword of sorrow would
pierce her heart when her son, her only son, would die on a
cross. But she would be there, faithful to the end and totally
obedient to God's will.

We know a few things about Jesus—son of God and son
of Mary, Savior of the world, and, yes, a sign of contradiction. Jesus was the revealing light to the Gentiles and the
glory of Israel. But for being the light, a light that exposed

deeds of darkness and human pretense, he would pay a price. He would be opposed because people opted for the darkness over the light lest their sins be exposed. But Jesus would be true to his mission and would offer redemption to a broken world.

Meditation: What do you know about Jesus and Mary? What values of theirs do you have within your heart?

Prayer: Jesus, son of Mary and prince of peace, help us to be true disciples. Like Simeon may we be just and open to your Spirit. Like Mary may we be faithful to God's will and willing to share in your suffering. And Lord, like you, may we be a light for others and, if need be, a sign of contradiction. When the sword of sorrow enters our life may we accept it with the same faith and trust that Mary had. Grant this in your mercy. Amen.

Vocation: Unique and Universal

Mass: 1 John 2:12-17; Luke 2:36-40

Scripture:
There was a certain prophetess, Anna by name, daughter of Phanuel of the tribe of Asher. . . . She was constantly in the temple, worshiping day and night in fasting and in prayer. (Luke 2:36-37)

Reflection: Each of us has our unique vocation determined by the gifts God has given us, the circumstances of our individual lives, and the stirrings of the Holy Spirit. Anna was called to be a prophetess as Mary was called to be the mother of Jesus. St. Paul had the vocation of bringing the message of Jesus to the Gentile world. Each of us is challenged to hear God's call and say yes.

Though our vocation is unique, there is something that is universal regarding our relationship with God. All of us, regardless of gender or geography or chronology, are to do what Anna did: pray and fast. In prayer we enter into that communication with God that sustains our spiritual life. It is all about listening and responding in a wonderful mutuality. God longs to speak to our hearts and to tell us of his love and mercy in Jesus. Anna prayed day and night giving thanks and praise to God.

Fasting is also part of everyone's vocation. Through discipline we make an effort to be free from things to be free for God. Fasting has a way of opening our minds and hearts to God's grace. All of us have to deal with areas of unfreedom in our lives, unfreedoms that often go by the name of addictions. Mortification, done under the inspiration of the Holy Spirit, sets us free to be open to God and to have energies to serve our sisters and brothers in need. Anna fulfilled both her individual and universal vocation.

Meditation: What role does personal prayer play in your life? Liturgical, public prayer? Do fasting and mortification have a place in your spirituality?

Prayer: God of the prophets and prophetesses, you call each of us by name. Help us to discern your call and to respond with courage and joy. You call all of us to be people of prayer, lifting our minds and hearts to you in deep faith and truth. We are also called to freedom. Send your Spirit of discipline into our lives so that we might avoid lives of self-indulgence and be for you and others. May we, like Jesus, grow in strength, wisdom, and grace. Amen.

December 31:
Seventh Day within the Octave of Christmas

Grace: Love Following upon Love

Mass: 1 John 2:18-21; John 1:1-18

Scripture:
John testified to him by proclaiming: "This is he of whom I said, 'The one who comes after me ranks ahead of me, for he was before me.'"
Of his fullness
we have all had a share—
love following upon love (John 1:15-16).

Reflection: Participation was one of the key words in Vatican Council II. In the document on the liturgy, the Council Fathers called us to full, conscious, active participation in our sacramental life. Here we have a share in the life of Jesus, the one witnessed to by John. We share in God's very life, what we call grace.

St. Augustine describes grace in these words: *"Quia amasti me, Domine, fecisti me amabilem"* ("Because you have loved me, O Lord, you have made me loveable"). This is to be understood in a twofold sense: being loved and able to love. Because of the mystery of the Incarnation, we are given a unique experience of God's love for us and are challenged to embrace that love and then give it away. "Love following upon love."

Reality demands that we confess to our lack of love. There is a meanness and cruelty in the human heart that too often is expressed in violence, hatred, and war. Instead of love following upon love, there is hatred following upon hatred. We need God's mercy and the healing presence of Jesus in the Eucharist to transform our hearts. To the extent that we open our lives to the transforming presence of Jesus will we participate and share in his glory. Impossible if left to our own resources; possible if the Spirit of Jesus is upon us.

Meditation: What is your level of participation in the life of Jesus and the Church? How open are you to the love offered in Christ?

Prayer: God of wisdom and love, you invite us to participate in the life, death, and resurrection of your Son, Jesus. May we say yes to this invitation and become committed disciples of Christ. Fill our hearts with your grace, your love, and help us to share that blessing with all whom we meet. Make us instruments and agents of your peace and joy in our day. We ask this in Jesus' name and give you thanks for your tender love. Amen.

JANUARY 1

The Heart of Mary

Mass: Num 6:22-27; Gal 4:4-7; Luke 2:16-21

Scripture:
Mary treasured all these things and reflected on them in
   her heart.
The shepherds returned, glorifying and praising God for
   all they had
heard and seen, in accord with what had been told them.
   (Luke 2:19-20)

Reflection: To know what goes on inside the heart of another is an intimate knowledge. Often we don't even know
what transpires within our own heart. But Mary knew. She
knew that God had entered her life with a special calling: to
conceive and bear Jesus. As we know from subsequent history, both joy and sorrow filled Mary's inner life.

Like the shepherds who were also graced with a special
revelation, Mary glorified and praised God for what he
was doing in her life. We have here one of the highest forms
of prayer. Unlike the prayer of thanksgiving or the prayer
of petition or the prayer of forgiveness, all of which involve
a huge portion of "self," the prayer of praise focuses on the
mystery of God. It is prayer of self-forgetfulness and recog-
nition of God's majesty.

Mary's heart was large. It contained not only reflections of God's marvelous deeds, but it also housed all she met. The shepherds were offered hospitality as were the disciples that Jesus would later call. Neighbors received a warm welcome as did strangers at the well. Mary's heart was more than reflective; it was a haven for all who needed to experience God's love.

Meditation: What goes on in your heart? How can we deepen our sense of hospitality, especially to the stranger?

Prayer: Gracious God, in Mary you have given us a model of true holiness. Hers was a loving heart, one rich in hospitality and prayerfulness. She responded fully to the call to be the mother of your Son and she was faithful to the end. Though at times her heart ached, she never allowed bitterness to reside there. Help us to be warmhearted people, a family committed to hospitality and service. Grant this through Mary's intercession. Amen.

EPIPHANY TO BAPTISM
OF THE LORD

January 2: Solemnity of the Epiphany

God's Self-Disclosure

Mass: Isa 60:1-6; Eph 3:2-3, 5-6; Matt 2:1-12

Scripture:
"Here is what the prophet has written:
    'And you, Bethlehem, land of Judah,
    are by no means least among the princes of Judah,
    since from you shall come a ruler
    who is to shepherd my people Israel.'" (Matt 2:5b-6)

Reflection: Epiphany! Manifestation! Showing! Revelation! What once was hidden has now come to light. In Jesus we have the self-disclosure of the mystery of God and the Gospel wonderfully presents this happening in stirring language. The star, the gifts, the Magi, the mother Mary, and even the wicked King Herod add drama to the greatest story of all time: God-become-man and made manifest in the child Jesus.

We too are to bring our gifts to this feast. Not the gifts of gold, frankincense, and myrrh, but the gifts of faith, hope, and love. For in Jesus we truly believe that God's love surrounds and sustains us; for in Jesus we have hope that God's promises of mercy and love will be fulfilled; for in Jesus we receive the love of the Father and commit ourselves to pass it on to others.

The manifestation of God in Jesus is startling. To be born in poverty under the circumstances of violence is disturbing for many. That an infinite God will take on our humanity, our suffering and death, seems incredible. That this ruler and shepherd would turn justice into mercy is almost too much to comprehend. On the feast we come in faith before a God of extravagant love and ask, once again, to be committed disciples of this loving Lord.

Meditation: What are some of the small and large epiphanies in your life? How has God revealed himself to you?

Prayer: God of wisdom and love, you come to us in so many ways. Through the gift of creation we marvel at your beauty and power. Through the gift of the Incarnation, the source of our redemption, we stand in awe. Continue to send your Spirit into our lives that we may recognize you in your many epiphanies, especially in your word and sacraments. Make us a eucharistic people, thankful for all your gifts, especially the gift of your Son Jesus. Amen.

God's Great Kingdom

Mass: 1 John 3:22–4:6; Matt 4:12-17, 23-25

Scripture:
From that time on Jesus began to proclaim this theme:
  "Reform your lives! The kingdom of heaven is at hand."
    (Matt 4:17)

Reflection: On the feast of Christ the King, the universal Church prays a special preface in which we hear that Jesus will one day present to the Father "an eternal and universal kingdom: a kingdom of truth and life, a kingdom of holiness and grace, a kingdom of justice, love, and peace."

The kingdom of God has seven markings: truth, life, holiness, grace, justice, love, and peace. In proclaiming this way of life Jesus calls for a reformation. For wherever there is the lie, or death dealing, or injustice, or hatred, or chaos the kingdom is being thwarted. In each of our lives we must name the demons that block us from doing God's will and bringing the kingdom to the place in which we live. As a pilgrim people we realize that we are on the way, a church of saints and sinners. Repentance and reformation must always be a part of our lives.

In our Gospel passage we see various phenomena that preclude the kingdom: John being arrested, a people living in darkness, so many diseases and illnesses, those possessed, the lunatics, the paralyzed. Jesus came to set free, to bring light, to bring love and life. He traveled far and wide to proclaim an alternative way of being and living. And then he sent forth others to continue his mission and ministry. And now he sends us.

Meditation: What do you understand by the "kingdom of God"? Which of the seven markings of the kingdom is most developed in your life, which the least?

Prayer: Lord Jesus, you have given us a great prayer in which we pray that God's will be done, God's kingdom might come. Empower us to be good evangelists, fearless in proclaiming your love and mercy. Enkindle us with your fiery Spirit that we may bring warmth and compassion to all we meet. Enlighten us to have a vision of what God's reign truly is and give us the grace of obedience to do whatever is asked of us. Grant this in your good mercy. Amen.

January 4: Tuesday after Epiphany

God's "Lunch"

Mass: 1 John 4:7-10; Mark 6:34-44

Scripture:
Then, taking the five loaves and two fish, Jesus raised his eyes to heaven, pronounced a blessing, broke the loaves, and gave them to the disciples to distribute. (Mark 6:41)

Reflection: Fr. Lawrence Jenco, a priest who was held hostage in the Middle East for almost two years, gave a college commencement address in which he told this story. The day his mother died she was trying to tell her son, Father Lawrence, something but because of her condition and all the tubes invading her body, he could not pick up her message, surely a message filled with some final words of wisdom. Finally, he heard her whisper: "Did you have lunch?" She died an hour later.

This was Jesus' concern as well. Were the people being fed, fed with physical food but also with spiritual nourishment. We have in the Gospel a feeding of bread and fish but also a feeding at a deeper level. Jesus knew well that the crowd and all of us hunger for meaning, hunger for integration, and hunger for intimacy.

It is through the Eucharist that these hungers are addressed. In God's word we are given meaning. Our lives are about service and compassion for others. Jesus tells us "to give them something to eat." We are here not to be served but to serve. In the Eucharist we pray for integration, for healing: "Lord, have mercy. Christ, have mercy. Lord, have mercy." Jesus came to put us back together again and free us from our sins and addictions. And the Eucharist is surely about intimacy, about communion. In approaching the altar we are nourished with the Body and Blood of the Lord. What a lunch we are given.

Meditation: What are the deepest hungers in your life? How does the Eucharist address these hungers? Whom are you asked to feed this day?

Prayer: Lord Jesus, we thank you for the gift of the Eucharist. In sharing yourself we are truly graced and set free. Our hungers are so many and deep. We tend to wander to resources other than you for satisfaction. Draw us back to you and help us to understand the mystery of your love in the sacraments. May we come to love your word more deeply and find it a source of meaning and hope. May we be healed of our brokenness so as to have energy to serve others. May we experience the intimacy of your tender mercies and rejoice with the communion of saints. We ask all this through your Spirit. Amen.

Fear Overcome

Mass: 1 John 4:11-18; Mark 6:45-52

Scripture:
He [Jesus] hastened to reassure them:
   "Get hold of yourselves! It is I.
   Do not be afraid!" (Mark 6:50)

Reflection: Understanding the meaning of events is a difficult enterprise. Be it the event of the multiplication of the loaves or the walking on water, be it the event of the news of terminal illness or unexplained remission, be it the news that war has been declared. Some events are historical, grounded in fact; other events are metaphorical, communicating a truth that demands symbols and images.

There is one event that is universal, historical, ubiquitous: the event of fear. We are rightly afraid of the dangers that surround us: nuclear threat, earthquakes and hurricanes, violence and brutality. Fear is the healthy and appropriate response to such events. Yet, fear must not govern our lives. It is there but so is the Lord, be it in the early hours of the morning or in the storms of our life or in the mystery of death. A sense of divine presence does not eliminate all fear but empowers us to be courageous in the midst of fear.

If we struggle to understand the complexity of life and its many ups and downs, we are in good company. The Twelve struggled as well: ". . . their minds were completely closed to the meaning of the events." It wasn't until the Spirit of Jesus transformed their minds and hearts that they began to see with the eyes of faith. And what they saw was the presence of a providential God who never abandons us. We are accompanied on this lifelong journey and it is that companionship that enables us to deal with the fears that inundate our lives.

Meditation: What fears do you have to contend with? How do you practice the presence of Jesus in your life?

Prayer: Loving God, you have sent your Son into the world to free us from sin and death. So often we are afraid of these mysteries and tremble before them. Help us to look upon your Son in faith, trusting that all will be well. In the storms of life come to us and give us courage. In the joys of life help us to be grateful and faithful to you. Through the gift of the Spirit may we truly understand the meaning of the events in our lives. Give us the gift of discernment; give us the gift of courage. We ask all this in Jesus' name. Amen.

The Mission of Jesus

Mass: 1 John 4:19–5:4; Luke 4:14-22

Scripture:
Then he [Jesus] began by saying to them:
   "Today this Scripture passage is fulfilled in your hearing."
      (Luke 4:21)

Reflection: To be clear about one's mission in life is a blessing. The great Cardinal Newman wrote a brutally honest prayer about *not* knowing exactly what the Lord is asking of us, but one day, in eternity, we will know. Many of us struggle to find our "niche," that area of life in which we can use our gifts most effectively in the service of others.

Jesus had a mission and he fulfilled it. The prophet Isaiah provides words to describe what God's work is through the gift of the Spirit: bringing glad tidings to the poor, proclaiming liberty and freedom to those held captive, giving sight to the blind, announcing a year of favor from the Lord. Here is the Christian job description. Through baptism and confirmation we are called into this way of life; through the Eucharist we are reminded of it and given the grace to live it. Hopefully we can say about our life that Isaiah's vision is being fulfilled in our times through the presence of Jesus working in our lives.

It is important to note that Jesus had the habit of going to the synagogue on the Sabbath. It is in public worship that we hear God's word, be it through the prophet Isaiah, the Psalms, the Gospels, or the writings of St. Paul. It is in church, the gathered community, that we hear God's word interpreted and applied to our lives. It is in the Christian assembly that Jesus comes to us with the grace to take the word and put it into action. Hearing is not enough; the word must be conceived and given birth.

Meditation: What is your mission statement? What is the work God has given you to do? Is that work being fulfilled? Today?

Prayer: God of word and sacrament, we thank and praise you for speaking to us through the Scriptures. Open our ears to your voice; open our eyes to your presence. May we not only hear your word but put it into practice. May our lives be good news to others; may we be concerned about setting people free through deeds of social justice; may we help others to see and hear your love. Through the gift of the Holy Spirit we will be able to translate your vision into history. Please, Lord, send that Spirit upon us this day. Amen.

"Be Cured!"

Mass: 1 John 5:5-13; Luke 5:12-16

Scripture:
Seeing Jesus, he [a man full of leprosy] bowed down to the ground and said to him:
"Lord, if you will to do so, you can cure me." (John 5:12)

Reflection: It was the psychologist Karl Jung who said that one third of his patients got worse, one third remained the same, and one third were "cured." Medical doctors probably have a similar batting average. Some illnesses are more susceptible to healing than others.

But when it comes to faith, we have barely tapped this great resource. The man with leprosy truly believed that Jesus could heal him. That faith, itself a gift, brought about a transformation that changed human destiny. Our faith challenges us to believe that, in Jesus, sin and death have been overcome. Sin and death! Two realities here that overwhelm our finite spirit. Yet Jesus broke the chains enslaving us to sin and has taken out the sting of death through the mystery of his resurrection.

Jesus wills to cure us. He came into the world that we might have fullness of life. Every illness and disease that diminishes life will be challenged by his Spirit. If we but see and hear Jesus, if we but feel this love and compassion, we too can be set free and rejoin the community, as the leper did, with tremendous joy and delight. Those glorious words: "Be cured!" are spoken to us today.

Meditation: In what ways has the Lord cured you? What illnesses still remain to be touched by the Lord?

Prayer: Compassionate and loving Jesus, we all suffer from our own unique leprosy. Come once again to heal us and restore us to community. For too long we have hidden from your gaze, have drawn back from your touch. Help us to see your compassionate heart and feel your merciful touch. Bring to our world, fractured by violence and war, your tender mercies. We ask this in and through the power of your Spirit. Amen.

January 8: Saturday after Epiphany

Increasing/Decreasing

Mass: 1 John 5:14-21; John 3:22-30

Scripture:
John answered:
 "He must increase,
  while I must decrease." (John 3:30)

Reflection: In his work *The Varieties of Religious Experience*, the psychologist William James states: "The saints are authors, *auctores*, increasers of goodness." Surely John the Baptist in his work of evangelization was an increaser of goodness and truth. Boldly he proclaimed the advent of God's kingdom and called people from darkness into the light. His prophetic mission and his commitment to God's will are evidence of the workings of grace.

But John speaks about decreasing in the Gospel today. The saint is also an author, *auctor*, a decreaser of one's own ego. One of the dangers of life in general and certainly of the spiritual life is that of narcissism. Saints must be conscious that the origin of goodness is God, not themselves. They are agents and instruments of goodness happening in particular times and places but are not themselves the font of truth and goodness. The underlying virtue that prevents egotism from getting a foothold is humility, the virtue that helps us to live in the truth of things. John's declaration of diminishment is grounded in a humble, truthful heart.

It is Jesus who must "increase," that is, become the center of our Christian journey. John knew that his mission was one of "preparing the way of the Lord," as predicted by his father. It would be through the forgiveness of sins and repentance that salvation would come. When his work was complete, John was willing to step aside. Here we find the true prophet, an increaser of both truth and goodness, a decreaser of pride and narcissism.

Meditation: In what ways do you increase goodness? To what extent is humility one of your prized virtues?

Prayer: Lord Jesus, in John the Baptist you found a loyal supporter. He prepared your way and opened the minds and hearts of people to your coming. Though bold and forceful in his preaching, he was humble of soul and knew well what his true mission was. Help us to live in humility, mindful that all truth and goodness come from you. Aid us as we proclaim your presence to the world and prevent us from living narcissistic lives. Free us from pride; grant us the grace of obedience. Grant this through the power of your Spirit. Amen.

January 9: Baptism of the Lord

Ongoing Baptism

Mass: Isa 42:1-4, 6-7; Acts 10:34-38; Matt 3:13-17

Scripture:
After Jesus was baptized,
  he came up from the water and behold,
  the heavens were opened for him,
  and he saw the Spirit of God descending like a dove
  and coming upon him.
And a voice came from the heavens, saying,
  "This is my beloved Son, with whom I am well pleased."
  (Matt 3:16-17)

Reflection: The mystery of baptism, that of Jesus and our own, deserves serious, prayerful reflection. What does it mean to plunge into these cleansing, sanctifying waters? How does baptism remain an ongoing reality in our lives so that it is not just a moment in time but a lifelong commitment to God's purposes? And how does baptism transform our lives so that now the Spirit has sway over our minds and hearts, over our cultures and our world?

Jesus did not shy away from participating in our human condition. Our sin he took upon himself and carried it into the salvific waters. From the inside Jesus felt our shame and guilt. He brought all of human history before God for purification and an infusion of grace. John the Baptist would be a mediator here and, though reluctant, yielded to the divine plan. Jesus was baptized and confirmed in the power of the Spirit. God was well pleased.

Every time we enter a church, we sign ourselves with baptismal waters. It not only reminds us that baptism continues to happen in our lives, it makes real this great sacrament here and now. Jesus comes to us with his healing power and longs to fill us with the power and grace of the Spirit. We need but open our minds and hearts to this invasion of grace.

Meditation: What does baptism mean to you? In what sense are baptism, confirmation, and marriage ongoing sacraments?

Prayer: Gracious God, in Jesus you give us life and love. In his baptism he began another phase of his mission to bring salvation to the world. We confess our sins; our guilt is indeed always before us. Send your Spirit into our lives that we may see your presence and respond to your call. As we come to the waters of the Jordan help us to know that we are pleasing in your sight. As we renew our baptism may we live more deeply lives of charity and justice. Grant this through Jesus, our Savior and friend. Amen.